I0813942

SPOTLIGHT ON GEORGIA

THE COLONIAL PERIOD OF GEORGIA'S HISTORY

SAM CROMPTON

NEW YORK

Published in 2018 by The Rosen Publishing Group, Inc.
29 East 21st Street, New York, NY 10010

Editor: Elizabeth Krajnik
Book Design: Rachel Rising

Photo Credits: Cover, p.23 MPI/Archive Photos/Getty Images; p. 5 Stock Montage/ Archive Photos/Getty Images; p. 6 https://commons.wikimedia.org/wiki/File:George_II_when_Prince_of_Wales.png; p. 7 https://commons.wikimedia.org/wiki/File:1747_Bowen_Map_of_the_Southeastern_United_States_(Carolina,_Georgia,_Florida)_-_Geographicus_-_CarolinaGeorgia-bowen-1747.jpg; p. 9 Jktu_21's/Shutterstock.com;p. 10 https://commons.wikimedia.org/wiki/File:Bulletin_(1901)_(19801833743).jpg; p. 11 Courtesy, Winterhur Museum, Painting, Audience Given by the Trustees of Georgia to a Delegation of Creek Indians; p. 13 Stephen Morton/Getty Images News/Getty Images; p. 14 https://de.wikipedia.org/wiki/Datei:SavannahCityPlan1770.jpg; p. 15 Courtesy of the Library of Congress; p. 16 https://commons.wikimedia.org/wiki/File:The_site_of_colonial_Fort_Augusta_behind_St._Paul's_Episcopal_Church..JPG; p.17 Visions of America/Universal Images Group/Getty Images; p. 18 meunierd/Shutterstock.com; p. 19 meunierd/Shutterstock.com; p. 20 https://commons.wikimedia.org/wiki/File:New_Ebenezer.jpg; p. 21 https://commons.wikimedia.org/wiki/File:Abp_Firmian_of_Salzburg.jpg; p. 25 Courtesy of the Allen County Public Library; p. 25 (background) Reinhold Leitner/Shutterstock.com; p. 27 https://commons.wikimedia.org/wiki/File:BloodyMarshMonument.jpg; p. 29 https://commons.wikimedia.org/wiki/File:CaptJohnReynolds.jpg.

Library of Congress Cataloging-in-Publication Data

Cataloging-in-Publication Data
Names: Crompton, Sam.
Title: The colonial period of Georgia's history / Sam Crompton.
Description: New York : PowerKids Press, 2018. | Series: Spotlight on Georgia | Includes index.
Identifiers: ISBN 9781508160113 (pbk.) | ISBN 9781508160144 (library bound) | ISBN 9781508160120 (6 pack)
Subjects: LCSH: Georgia--History--Colonial period, ca. 1600-1775--Juvenile literature.
Classification: LCC F289.C76 2018 | DDC 975.8'02--dc23

Manufactured in the United States of America

CPSIA Compliance Information: Batch #BS17PK For further information contact Rosen Publishing, New York, New York at 1-800-237-9932.

CONTENTS

CHAPTER ONE

THE FIRST STEPS TOWARD COLONIZATION

The United States of America wasn't always an independent country. It was originally made up of 13 British colonies. In 1733, Georgia became the 13th colony established in North America. The story of Georgia began in 1729, when a man named James Oglethorpe started working to **reform** prisons in London, England. These prisons were filled with people who were in debt. The conditions were terrible.

Oglethorpe had some success with prison reform, but there were still many poor people in England. Oglethorpe and some of his fellow reformers decided to start a new colony in America in which some of England's poor could start over.

England and the earlier 12 colonies had many issues with the divide between the rich and poor. To avoid this in the new colony, Oglethorpe and the others created rules that said the settlers wouldn't be allowed to own large plots of land or have slaves.

James Oglethorpe decided to reform London's prisons after his friend Robert Castell was imprisoned because of debt. Castell later died of **smallpox**, which he caught from his cellmate.

CHAPTER TWO

THE CHARTER OF 1732

To start a colony, Oglethorpe had to get approval for a **charter** from King George II and British Parliament. This charter was granted in early 1732. The new colony was named after the king. It was established between the Savannah and Altamaha Rivers.

KING GEORGE II

Although Oglethorpe originally wanted people who had been in prison for debt to colonize Georgia, the trustees chose people who would be able to make the colony successful, such as carpenters, farmers, and merchants. This map from 1747 shows the colonies of Georgia and the Carolinas.

Georgia's charter contained a number of rules for the new colony. Colonists had the same rights as English citizens, but could not form a local government. People living in the colony could practice their religion freely—unless they were Roman Catholic or Jewish.

Oglethorpe and 20 other people acted as the first **trustees**. They were responsible for making decisions and taking care of the new colony. These trustees governed Georgia for the first 20 years of the colony's history. To pick the first colonists, the trustees interviewed people who wanted to move to Georgia.

CHAPTER THREE

SETTLING IN GEORGIA

While Oglethorpe originally wanted the new colony to be a way to help London's poor and indebted people, there were two other important reasons for colonizing Georgia.

The Georgia colony was located between the colony of South Carolina to the north, Spanish Florida to the south, and French Louisiana to the west. The new colony gave South Carolina protection from possible threats from the Spanish and French, both of whom had **allies** among the **indigenous** peoples of the area.

Most of the more than 3,000 people who eventually **immigrated** to the new colony received funding from Georgia's trustees. They received the fare for their passage, enough food and supplies for one year, and a plot of land. All of these things were given to the colonists in return for their labor.

VIRGINIA

NEW FRANCE

NORTH CAROLINA

CEDED FROM SOUTH CAROLINA TO GEORGIA IN 1787

SOUTH CAROLINA

1732 CHARTER BOUNDARY

SAVANNAH R.

GEORGIA

DISPUTED WITH SPAIN UNTIL 1795

ALTAMAHA R.

GEORGIA EXPANDED SOUTH OF THE ALTAMAHA IN 1763

WEST FLORIDA

EAST FLORIDA

South Carolina was a valuable and important colony. Georgia's location was chosen because of this. This map shows how Georgia's boundaries changed during the 1700s

CHAPTER FOUR

TWO IMPORTANT FRIENDS

When Oglethorpe and the colonists arrived in Georgia in early 1733, they were not the first people to settle there. People had been living in Georgia and the surrounding areas for hundreds of years before European explorers arrived. These explorers required translators and **mediators** to make sure that their relationships with these indigenous people remained peaceful.

TOMOCHICHI

Tomochichi wanted the Georgia trustees to recognize that his people had rights and fought for fair trade. This painting shows Oglethorpe presenting Tomochichi and other Yamacraw people to Georgia's trustees in England.

One important player in the relations between the English settlers and Georgia's indigenous people was Tomochichi, the chief of the Yamacraw people. Oglethorpe consulted Tomochichi about Savannah's planning and fair **negotiations** with neighboring groups of indigenous peoples. Tomochichi had met settlers in South Carolina and was very important to Georgia's success as a colony. Oglethorpe viewed Tomochichi as a friend.

A year after the colonists arrived, Tomochichi and some of his people voyaged to England with Oglethorpe. They met with King George II and spoke for their people.

Mary Musgrove was another important person in the English settlers' interactions with the people of Georgia. Musgrove, or Coosaponakeesa, was the daughter of Edward Griffin—an Englishman—and a Creek woman. She spoke both English and the Creek language of Muskogee and served as an interpreter for Oglethorpe from 1733 to 1743. Her knowledge of indigenous and colonial ways made her very helpful to Oglethorpe and Tomochichi.

In addition to being a diplomat, Musgrove was also a knowledgeable businesswoman. She and her first husband, John Musgrove, married in 1717 and set up a trading post where Musgrove helped her husband as an interpreter. Her knowledge of language and ways of life likely attracted many customers. John Musgrove accompanied Oglethorpe on his journey to England in 1734. Afterward, the trustees granted him a plot of land on Yamacraw Bluff just outside Savannah.

In 2002, archaeologists unearthed Mary Musgrove's second trading post, known as the Cowpens, which sits on Yamacraw Bluff. This trading post was a booming center for the deerskin trade in colonial Georgia.

CHAPTER FIVE

THE TOWN OF SAVANNAH

Without the knowledge and experience of Tomochichi and Mary Musgrove, Savannah's establishment would have gone differently. Oglethorpe founded Savannah according to the rules of Georgia's trustees in England.

Savannah was laid out like a grid with wide streets and public squares. There were originally 24 squares, but only 22 remain today. This type of layout had not been used before in the colonies, making Savannah one of America's first planned cities. It was intended to look similar to a London town model with several variations.

SAVANNAH CITY PLAN

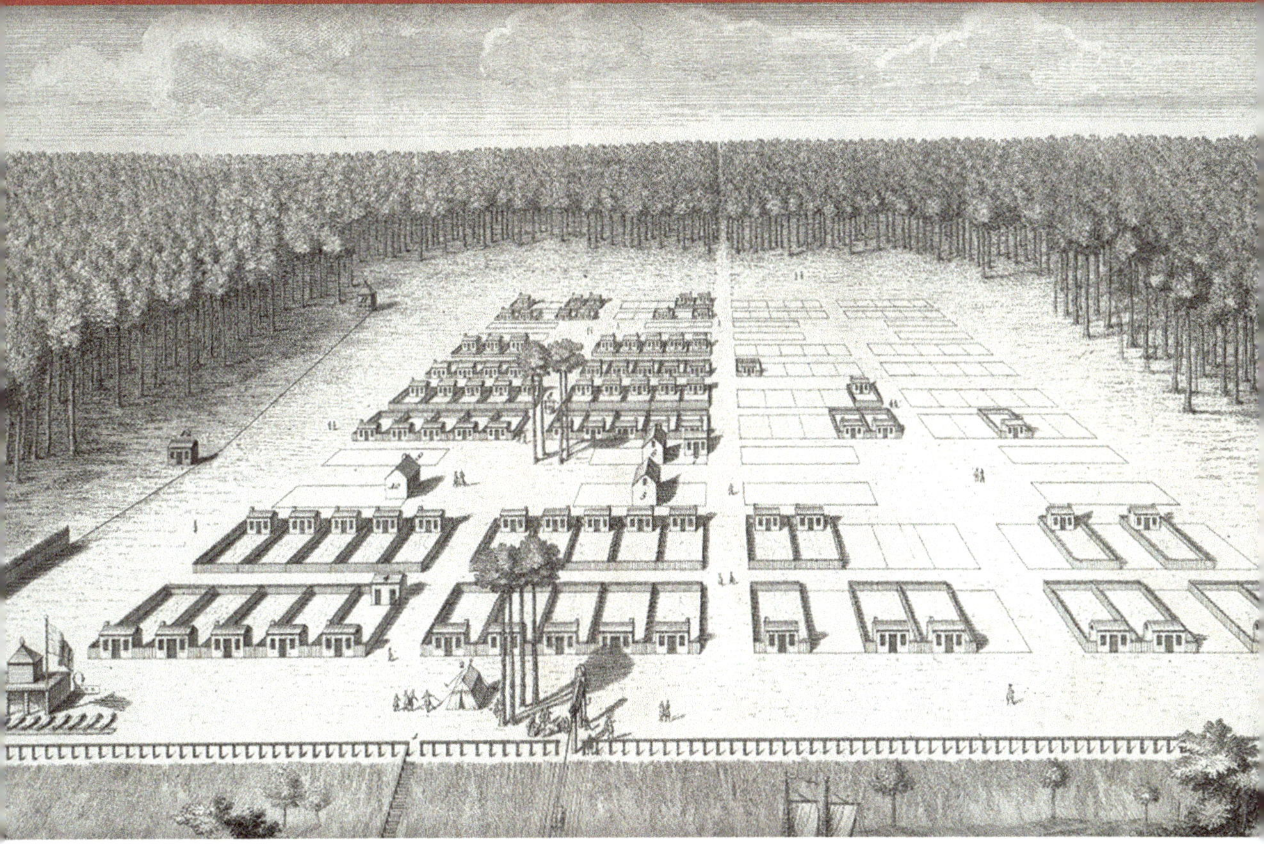

Savannah's grid-like city plan allowed for more green space to be used as gardens and farm lots. The uniform sizes of the lots reflect the ideal of equal sharing among colonists.

The trustees' many rules affected the colonists' daily lives. Slavery and certain types of alcohol were banned. Catholics were not allowed to live in the colony. However, Savannah's population was made up of people from many different backgrounds. People from across western Europe came to settle in the new colony.

CHAPTER SIX

SPREADING OUT

After Oglethorpe successfully established Savannah, he wanted to spread out and create cities in other parts of Georgia. He ordered forts to be built to protect Savannah and South Carolina from the Spanish, French, and indigenous people. The first of these forts was Fort Argyle. Fort Augusta, Fort Frederica, and Fort Saint Simon were built soon after Fort Argyle was built.

FORT AUGUSTA MONUMENT

All that's left of Fort Augusta is Saint Paul's Episcopal Church, which sat just outside the walls of the fort. The Fort Augusta Monument marks the site of the former fort.

Fort Augusta, now the city of Augusta, was originally an important trading post. Many traders stopped there on their travels farther southeast. Oglethorpe recognized that the location of the trading post would be a perfect place to build a fort. He gave builders permission to start Fort Augusta's construction in 1735. It was not completed until 1739.

Oglethorpe used this fort as a meeting place. In 1739, he met with the leaders of the Cherokee and Chickasaw people to discuss a smallpox outbreak. This meeting prevented a war from starting.

CHAPTER SEVEN

JEWISH SETTLERS IN GEORGIA

During colonial times, Georgia was home to a **diverse** population. After the English settlers arrived in Georgia in early 1733, a group of 42 Jewish settlers landed in Savannah on July 11, 1733. Oglethorpe had not expected the presence of the Jewish settlers, but they were allowed to stay and lived together in harmony.

Oglethorpe was pleased to learn that one of the members of this group of new settlers was a doctor. Samuel Nunes provided medical attention to many of Georgia's settlers allowing them to survive their first year in the colony.

In July 1735, Benjamin Sheftall and his sons, who were **Ashkenazic Jews**, helped establish the Congregation Mickve Israel, or Hope of Israel. Before this, the Jewish settlers probably practiced their faith in the homes of their peers rather than in a synagogue, or a Jewish house of worship.

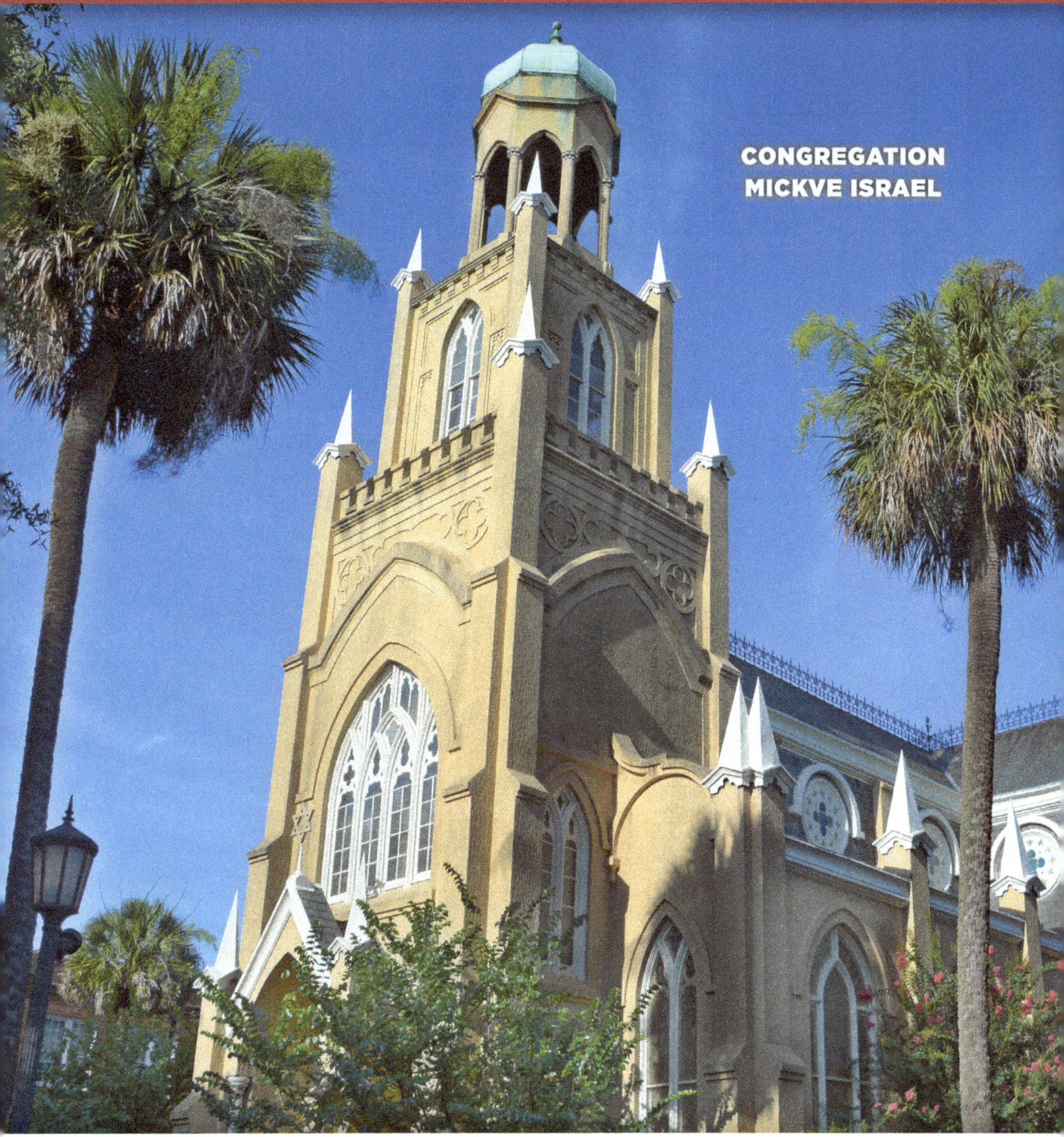

CONGREGATION MICKVE ISRAEL

While living in Europe, many **Sephardic Jews** practiced Roman Catholicism in public and Judaism in private. Religious freedom was one of many reasons people chose to immigrate to the British colonies in America.

CHAPTER EIGHT

EXILED FROM SALZBURG

Jews were not the only people who sought religious safety in the new colony. In 1734, the Salzburgers, a group of German-speaking **Protestants** from Salzburg, which is in present-day Austria, arrived in Georgia. They had been forced from their home and sought the help of King George II and the Georgia trustees.

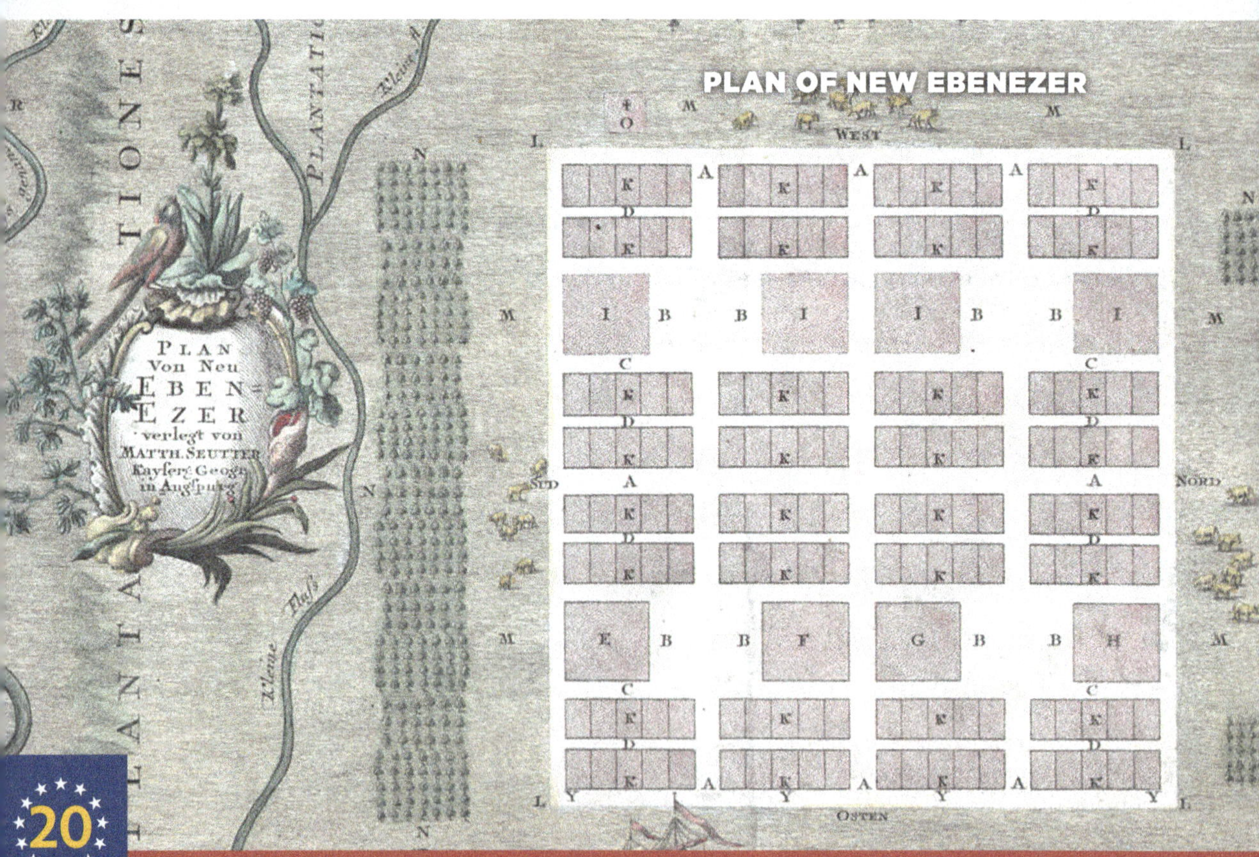

PLAN OF NEW EBENEZER

Archbishop Leopold von Firmian, shown here, forced the Protestant Salzburgers out of their country because they refused to convert to Catholicism. These people settled in several countries surrounding present-day Austria as well as in the colony of Georgia.

The Salzburgers landed in Charleston, South Carolina, on March 7, 1734. When they arrived in Savannah, Oglethorpe directed them to an area of land where they founded the town of Ebenezer, which means "stone of help" in Hebrew. These people made the best of their situation and founded their town with strong religious values.

However, this settlement was not successful. The soil was infertile and many settlers died from sickness. The Salzburgers asked Oglethorpe for permission to move the town. They founded New Ebenezer, which shared a similar layout with Savannah.

CHAPTER NINE

THE SCOTS OF DARIEN

On October 18, 1735, a group of Scottish Highlanders from Inverness, Scotland, set sail for Georgia. They arrived on January 19, 1736, and founded New Inverness, later renamed Darien. Like the other groups of colonists, the Scottish settlers brought their religious beliefs with them. They introduced Presbyterianism, a type of Protestantism, to the colony.

Upon their arrival, the Scottish settlers replaced Fort King George, which had been built to protect the area from the Spanish. Fort King George was abandoned in 1732. The Scottish colonists were known for their strength and bravery and had been encouraged to immigrate to Georgia to help defend the colony from the ever-increasing threat of the Spanish to the south. The Highlanders were not bothered by the possibility of Spanish attack and established Darien in spite of the warnings from South Carolina settlers.

James Oglethorpe was very impressed with the Highlanders' culture. When he visited Darien, he wore Highlander clothing and slept outside with them.

CHAPTER TEN

GEORGIA'S MALCONTENTS

Throughout Georgia's trustee period, a number of colonists were very open about their displeasure with the people in charge of governing the colony. These people were known as Malcontents. Some of the rules they opposed most strongly were limits on how much land the colonists could own, the ban on slavery, and the ban on certain types of alcohol.

Patrick Tailfer and Thomas Stephens led the group of Malcontents. In 1738, the Malcontents made an official complaint about how the colony was being governed, but the trustees did not respond to their **petition**. As a result, many Malcontents left the colony in 1740.

The trustees claimed that they were well liked among the majority of the colonists and said they would not make any changes to how things were run. Tailfer responded that Georgia would not be a successful colony if the trustees didn't change their rules.

A TRUE AND HISTORICAL

NARRATIVE

OF THE

COLONY OF GEORGIA

IN AMERICA,

From the First Settlement Thereof until this Present Period.
Containing the most Authentic Facts, Matters, and
Transactions therein; together with his Majesty's
Charter, Representations of the People,
Letters, etc., and a

DEDICATION TO HIS EXCELLENCY GENERAL OGLETHORPE.

BY

PAT. TAILFER, M. D.,
HUGH ANDERSON, M. A.,
DA. DOUGLAS, AND OTHERS,
Landholders in Georgia, at present in Charles-Town in
South Carolina.

——Qui Deorum
Muneribus sapienter uti,
Duramq; callet Pauperiemq; pati,
Pejusq; Letho Flagitium timer,
Non ille pro caris Amicis
Aut Patria timidus Perire. H. 4 O.

CHARLES-TOWN, SOUTH CAROLINA:
Printed by P. TIMOTHY, for the Authors,
1741.

Tailfer responded to William Stephens's memorial with a document entitled *A True and Historical Narrative of the Colony of Georgia*. This document claimed that the trustees' policies made it hard for the colonists to succeed in Georgia.

CHAPTER ELEVEN

THE SPANISH THREATEN GEORGIA

The Spanish were an ever-present threat to the colonists in Georgia. The English and Spanish had been fighting over the land that was now Georgia for over two centuries. In late 1739, this fighting turned into the War of Jenkins' Ear.

Oglethorpe and other men from Georgia invaded Florida in January 1740, seizing two Spanish forts, both of which were near Saint Augustine. In May 1740, he unsuccessfully attempted to take the fort at Saint Augustine. This siege sparked the Spanish to lead an invasion of Georgia.

About 5,000 Spanish soldiers entered Georgia in mid-June 1742. On July 7, 1742, the Spanish and the colonists from Georgia fought on Saint Simons Island. This battle became known as the Battle of Bloody Marsh. This was the first time the Spanish attempted to invade Georgia. Oglethorpe and his 1,000 men defeated the Spanish, who left the island on July 13.

The Spanish defeat at Saint Simons Island discouraged them from attacking Georgia again. Today, a marker sits at the site of the Battle of Bloody Marsh in honor of the lives that were lost there.

CHAPTER TWELVE

GEORGIA BECOMES A ROYAL COLONY

In 1752, Georgia's trustees turned the colony back over to the British government. From 1752 to 1754, there was a limited government in the colony while its new charter was being approved by British Parliament and signed by the king. Upon the charter's approval, Parliament appointed a governor to make decisions for the colony.

Georgia's first royal governor, John Reynolds, arrived in Savannah on October 29, 1754. Although Reynolds had experience with Britain's navy, he wasn't particularly well suited to politics. He was able to make some of the changes that the colonists had requested. However, Reynolds wasn't a good leader and many of his council members challenged his authority. Reynolds responded by trying to take complete control of the government. The British government told Reynolds to return to England and turned the colony over to Henry Ellis on February 16, 1757.

John Reynolds, shown here, went back to England and continued life with Britain's navy, eventually reaching the rank of full admiral. His brief time as Georgia's first royal governor caused many problems in the colony such as financial hardship and caused Georgia to be unappealing to future immigrants.

CHAPTER THIRTEEN

A RISING REVOLUTION

After the French and Indian War ended in 1763, Georgia gained a great deal of land. This land needed settlers, so the colonial government created two new townships. In 1773, the Creek and Cherokee peoples sold some of their land in the area to the colony. James Wright, Georgia's third royal governor, claimed that these lands were ideal areas for settlement because they were farther away from New England, where many colonist uprisings were happening.

Political unrest existed in the colonies before the Revolutionary War began. With the Stamp Act of 1765, Parliament attempted to raise money by taxing much of the colonies' printed material. Many of the colonists opposed this act and it was repealed. But problems continued to exist between Britain and its colonies and would eventually result in war.

GLOSSARY

ally (AA-ly) A person or country associated with another for a common purpose.

Ashkenazic Jew (aash-kuh-NAA-zihk JOO) A person who belongs to the subgroup of Jews descended from those from France, Germany, and Eastern Europe.

charter (CHAR-tuhr) A document issued by a government that gives rights to a person or group.

diverse (dih-VERS) Having many different types, forms, or ideas.

immigrate (IH-muh-grayt) To come to a country to live there.

indigenous (in-DIH-juh-nuhs) Having started in and coming naturally from a certain area.

mediator (MEE-dee-ay-tuhr) A person who works with two people to get them to agree.

negotiation (nih-go-shee-AY-shun) A formal discussion between people who are trying to reach an agreement.

petition (puh-TIH-shun) A formal written request to a leader or government regarding a particular issue.

Protestant (PRAH-tuhs-tuhnt) A member of one of the Christian churches that separated from the Roman Catholic Church in the 16th century.

reform (ree-FORM) The improvement of something by removing faults or problems.

Sephardic Jew (suh-FAR-dik JOO) A person who belongs to the subgroup of Jews descended from those from Spain, Portugal, North Africa, and the Middle East.

smallpox (SMAL-pahks) A serious disease that causes fever and a rash and often death.

trustee (truhs-TEE) A person who has been given legal responsibility for someone else's property.

INDEX

PRIMARY SOURCE LIST

Page 11

Audience Given by the Trustees of Georgia to a Delegation of Creek Indians. Painting. Created by William Verelst. Published in London ca. 1734–1735. Now kept at the Winterthur Museum, Garden & Library, Winterthur, Delaware.

Page 15

A view of Savanah [sic] as it stood the 29th of March, 1734. Engraving. Created by Fourdrinier, P. Published in London ca. 1735. Now kept at the Library of Congress Prints and Photographs Division, Washington, D.C.

Page 25

A True and Historical Narrative of the Colony of Georgia, in America, from the First Settlement Thereof until this Present Period. Created by Patrick Tailfer, Hugh Anderson, David Douglas, and others. Published in Charles-Town, South Carolina. Printed by P. Timothy in 1741. Now kept at the Allen County Public Library Genealogy Center in Fort Wayne, Indiana.

WEBSITES

Due to the changing nature of Internet links, PowerKids Press has developed an online list of websites related to the subject of this book. This site is updated regularly. Please use this link to access the list: www.powerkidslinks.com/sog/colonial